Tarot

Learn How to Read Tarot Cards for Divination

(Everything You Need to Know to Harness the Wisdom of the Cards)

Daniel Cannon

Published By **Tyson Maxwell**

Daniel Cannon

Tarot: Learn How to Read Tarot Cards for Divination (Everything You Need to Know to Harness the Wisdom of the Cards)

ISBN 978-1-998927-12-8

Legal & Disclaimer

Table Of Contents

Chapter 1: THE MAJOR ARCANA

These ordinary archetypes take you on a adventure through life. The visitor is the card numbered 0, the Fool.

The Fool, Major Arcana Card #zero

In Tarot, the Fool is the card numbered zero because of the truth they're the entirety and not anything. They can become whatever as they set out on their journey to self-popularity, via the Major Arcana playing gambling playing cards. They launch into the void, step off a precipice, or encompass the instincts in their animal accomplice, and embark on the adventure of life, represented by the usage of manner of the Major Arcana.

The Fool has no gender and no specific girl or masculine power, just an insatiable urge for meals for brand new enjoy and for shelling out consciousness from humor, simplicity, or madness.

The Fool is privy to that to admit lack of knowledge is the very excellent knowledge due to the reality that's when you test what you don't understand and that each starting is an opportunity. They comprehend that laughter keeps us transferring, that taking ourselves too significantly is deadly, that appearances can be deceiving, and that a prank or two maintains us on our toes. They are the clean slate wherein the solution to any question may be written. In a analyzing, the Fool almost constantly says, "Go for it!". Reversed (the other way up) technique perhaps you're no longer listening for that first step.

THE MAGICIAN.

The Magician, Major Arcana Card #1

The Magician is putting in the circle of the four fits, the committed location wherein magic can rise up. This card, like many, has lengthy beyond via a alternate for the purpose that early days of Tarot centuries in the past.

Today, the Magician is visible on top of things, serene and powerful, drawing magic down with tool that often include the raised wand, the four factors, and the infinity sign that hovers above them. Earlier decks depicted a trickster of kinds, a con-artist, a jester and juggler working in the direction of sleight-of-hand. Depending on the context, it could nonetheless be each.

In a analyzing, this card represents willful transformation, consciously directing and manipulating energy. It's an auspicious card for creatives. This IS creativity itself. Reversed, we want to test out for the desire have come to be to damaging or egocentric capabilities, or progressive strength disrupted or blocked. It's huge juju, however it falls.

The High Priestess, Major Arcana Card #2

The High Priestess consists of instinct, dream, and vision. This is the personification of thriller who whispers together along with your internal voice. In early decks, she become La Papesse, the girl pope, that which end up hidden in reality. Legends of Pope Joan aside, we see time and again that the idea of the divine female will discover its way into the tales and humanities of even the maximum patriarchal cultures. Feminine strength swirls and spirals. Masculine electricity is linear. We all deliver severa portions of both.

In maximum decks, she sits earlier than the curtain, the veil, and some of the pillars of mild and darkness. She nearly normally sits with multiple symbols of female energy: the moon, the pomegranate, and every so often a snake or owl. In a reading, she reminds us to however our mind chatter and pay attention. Just pay attention.

THE EMPRESS.

The Empress, Major Arcana Card #3

The Queen of the Tarot deck represents fertility and abundance. She is pregnant with all this is born, grown, or created. Three is the kind of compelling huge variety – there are trinities anywhere inside the perception structures and mythologies of the area. One plus equals three, that it's born. Whenever you look at a three in a reading, some thing new is starting, a few element is being created.

Life-giving female strength is the large message that consists of this card. Motherhood in all its office paintings – ardour and creativity. Reversed, the Empress can be stagnant, no longer growing, not playing, and no longer growing.

The Emperor, Major Arcana Card #4

This picture is all approximately structure and limitations. It includes linear, masculine strength. It's temporal power, authority, and experience which could carry information. This is the daddy, the builder, the king of the Major Arcana, because the Empress is the mother and queen. He consists of no weapon, simply the sigils of power – the orb, the shield, and the team of workers.

In a studying, this photo regularly shows a courting in the norms of society, obedience to policies, felony tips, customs, and expectancies of conformity (or the patriarchal yoke, relying on how you have a look at it). He is domineering, and he may be benevolent or tyrannical. Reversed, he softens, and can consist of recognition or maybe inclined aspect. Always, this card represents the more criminal tips of shape and life.

THE HIEROPHANT

The Hierophant, Major Arcana Card #five

Behold the keeper of tradition and of secrets and techniques and strategies and strategies. This parent changed into as quickly as

8

represented because the Pope in older decks. Today, we normally consider the Hierophant because of the fact the purveyor of ordinary or installation know-how in the exoteric or outer international, in preference to the High Priestess' esoteric, internal, or mystery knowledge that calls on instinct and dream.

The phrase Hierophant manner "he who indicates," so this determine is a trainer, a mentor, probably a guru. In a analyzing, he can represent an educational revel in or an enterprise of a few type. In some contexts, you could see a benediction or blessing with the useful resource of a respected superior or leader. Reversed, the Hierophant shows a rejection of an predicted course or notion – unorthodoxy.

The Lovers, Major Arcana Card #6

This card, a chunk counter-intuitively, is all approximately desire. You might also, reflexively, see romantic love right here, and every so often that's what it is, however no longer constantly thru any manner. In fact, all sixes in the Tarot deck are about selecting a few trouble. Here, we're asking, "What is The Beloved?"

In many modern-day-day decks, this card depicts romantic love, and that's the first layer, the easy which means that, however there's more. The Beloved can be a associate or soul mate, but can also, at any given time, be a mission, a place, a adventure, a notion, a puppy – a few aspect lighting you up at that factor. The wonderful playing cards inside the layout impart the context. If the card is reversed, it can advocate NOT love, or it could allow you to recognize which you want to count on more difficult about a preference you're making and be more planned in selecting a path.

The Chariot, Major Arcana Card #7

Welcome to the procession. It's a parade float! This card comes from the oldest, deep levels of Tarot. It's a triomf or triumph, a show that traveled in a cart or an real chariot, often to have fun a victory. Sometimes, it changed into a tableau that didn't go with the flow in any respect. The practice is going once more as a minimum to Roman instances.

A seven is constantly about getting organized for motion, studying, and planning. Display, motion within stillness. It's a sacred range: seven planetary spheres, seven musical notes, seven chakras, seven colorations of the rainbow.

In a studying, look for success that comes from exerting your will to the admiration of others. Reversed, it may endorse the quit of keeping some thing that takes incredible attempt - the selection (the revel in, the adventure) fails or is intentionally withdrawn. The chariot is a vehicle to maintain us thru in a stately, ordered, perambulation.

Strength, Major Arcana Card #8

This card has modified masses through the years. First, it was once #eleven and come to be repositioned by using way of manner of the Golden Dawn early within the 20th century, in massive factor for astrological alignment with Leo. You'll in spite of the fact that every so often find decks in which Justice is #eight and Strength is #11, but in favored, the trade has caught.

The meaning has also morphed. Strength changed into frequently (and though is now and again) interpreted as overcoming preference or ardour or animal nature. But masses of us have a observe passion in every other manner these days and at the whole no longer as some component to be tamed. Strength is now regularly visible as fortitude, braveness, believe, and self-self guarantee or personal will in preference to stress. Love, even. I count on this card is based upon on the others round it in a analyzing, and the manner querents define electricity for themselves. Reversed, it way...Properly, the exact opposite, or weakened power.

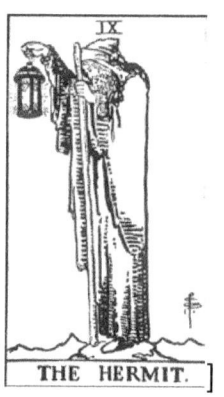

The Hermit, Major Arcana Card #9

This is one of the greater clear-cut archetypal gambling gambling cards, regardless of the fact that there's lots to meditate on right here, too —and that's kind of the factor. We see the Wise One, who is alone, reclusive, or emotionally apart, trying to find enlightenment. The seeker, the shaman, the curandera, the guru, who has come via their expertise right now...and by myself. That's the primary layer.

Many figures of the Hermit have a moderate, a lantern, a candle, a torch, a few element lighting the way to bring a few thing statistics and know-how they've got accumulated decrease lower lower back to the area with the slight of affection, compassion, and heat. Reconnecting is the second layer.

In a studying, the advice can be to spend time by myself, to retreat and hook up with your inner voice and the herbal worldwide. Depending on the location and surrounding playing cards, it can additionally remind you that an excessive amount of seclusion can result in loneliness and a want to hook up with others. That sounds acquainted, doesn't it? And the range nine – 3 times three is a effective enormous form of entirety and hundreds. Whatever we're coping with, there's lots of it, and we've located plenty approximately it. Time to ponder.

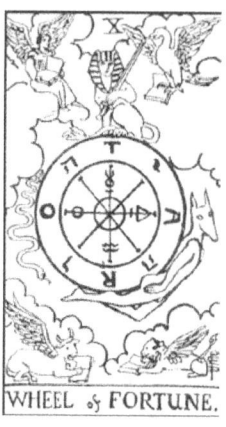

The Wheel of Fortune, Major Arcana card #10

"What is going up ought to come down" or "what goes round comes around." Just approximately the whole thing we comprehend within the herbal international is cyclical. This is an picture that humans may additionally have diagnosed at least as a ways again because the Medieval period in Europe. But that's now not all. It's a subject matter commonplace to pretty masses all cultures and notion systems. It no longer quality represents the cycle of Fortune, but also the cycles of time or maybe reincarnation. It's clean to see the wheel of the twelve months and its seasonal celebrations, in addition to fickle destiny, spinning round stillness at the middle. We see the forces of existence.

The massive variety ten reduces to at least one, just like the Magician who wields all the factors, so this is some element given, a few component at the begin, some detail primal.

In a studying, we normally see this card as true exact fortune besides it's surrounded via way of playing playing cards that display a reversal. Upright is upward, reversed is downward. Spin the wheel and take - or make - your possibilities!

Justice, Major Arcana card #11

The Justice card is all about balance. It comes exactly within the center of the Fool's journey via the primary gambling cards – ten playing gambling cards in advance than and ten cards after. This seems becoming for a card that often includes an image of blindfolded Justice with balanced scales, the older decks based on the Greek goddess, Themis. That balance because the midpoint card is one of the primary motives that this card grow to be renumbered through way of the Golden Dawn in the early 20th century. I cited this in #8 – Strength. The cards switched places.

Justice is typically look at as balance in appropriate reward or punishment for moves. A really global method honesty and appreciate, equity and opportunity, examining relationships and transactions for equity. Balancing the beyond and the future inside the gift is likewise a recurring topic with this card. The idea of Justice also has been used to scare human beings into obedience to a predetermined set of guidelines. The card isn't always frequently observe that manner in recent times – it's greater approximately analyzing your very private dealings with the arena for reality. Right factor up, it shows a sincere and without a doubt quit result. Reversed, not loads.

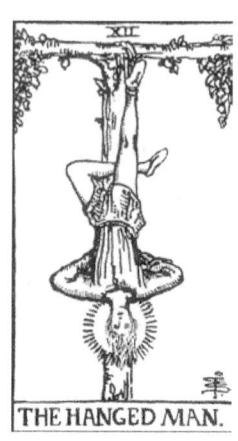

THE HANGED MAN.

The Hanged Man, Major Arcana card #12

First, I need to exchange this to The Hanged One. In modern decks, the discern putting the opportunity way up is any gender, and the power of the card isn't precise. This is one of the most talked about playing gambling cards within the Tarot and one of the most placing. Is it about betrayal? Sacrifice? Stagnation? Suffering? Punishment? Contemplation? Renunciation? Circumspection? Trials? Prophecy? You will find a reader someplace who will recollect any of these interpretations.

I think it's approximately initiation which could glide over into any of those one in every of a type meanings– seeing matters from a new angle. I think about Odin placing the other way up at the tree of information, a willing sufferer, open to receiving expertise. I don't forget how infants were born the opposite manner up for millennia earlier than women started out lying all the way down to offer beginning.

I reflect onconsideration on the card's variety, twelve: a one and a , which mixes the Magician and the High Priestess – seen and invisible notion. That makes it a 3, that effective trinity or triad, that indicates beginnings, harmony, bringing matters together. If the Hanged One is stuck, I suppose it's for the purpose of finding a trendy angle, soaking up what's essential to have a have a study and studies. Reversed, perhaps they need to pay more attention to instinct and plenty much less to the babble round them.

Death, Major Arcana card #13

Now proper right here's a card that's feared and misunderstood – and dramatized. The killer leaves a Death card with their sufferer, and the detective grimaces at the supernatural turn the case has taken. The fortune teller pulls the Death card, and the track swells. Does Death suggest lack of existence? Occasionally, however it can moreover suggest that the querent is handling bodily loss of life as an hassle of their existence, a dominant challenge remember on the time of the analyzing or meditation on the cardboard. Once, that come to be quite an awful lot the nice that means of the card; death, corruption, destruction, mortality.

In the remaining century, the which means that shifted to be more about profound modifications of a big range and new starting. We're no longer talking approximately a floor alternate or transition of 1 issue to seem like a few element else, however real transformation – an finishing that results in the beginning of some factor completely outstanding. Something ends and, to a point, that looks as if a loss of existence. Maybe it's the loss of life or eliminating of a dating, or process, or attachment to a specific vicinity, or part of the ego that now not identifies or serves you. It isn't constantly sad and frequently opens the way for some thing new to be born. Reversed, it could advocate a change this is stalled.

The Death card is, of course, extensive variety 13. The moon has 13 cycles and is born and dies all through every of them. There are twelve astrological signs and symptoms and signs and symptoms and what lies beyond? Judas became the thirteenth character at the Last Supper. Loki the Trickster became the thirteenth traveller at Odin's table. You can locate extra correspondences in hundreds of cultures and beliefs. One plus three equals 4, the variety of shape, boundaries, and bounds. Death limits all and is a boundary, a gateway.

Temperance, Major Arcana card #14

The top layer of Temperance is set moderation and restraint, calm and balance. Tempering wine as quickly as supposed mixing it with water to lessen its performance. The Temperance Movement drew on the ones ideas and Prohibition befell within the United States. When you mood steel, you warm temperature it to make it sturdy but now not brittle –within the path of the approach, it's malleable, but no longer heated to the factor in which it's molten. Medieval era taught that the frame contained humors or tempers that wished balance to preserve fitness. When you "lose your mood," you lose that balance.

The next layer of because of this is combining elements. The Temperance card depicts an angel or special magical being, frequently winged, combining factors, pouring liquid from one vessel to each different at angles that defy gravity. They are typically status in the world and water. Their wings are often too large for the body. Mixing. Alchemy. Combining elements to make a few factor precise pop out the opportunity prevent. Mixed in a wonderful manner, there's a extraordinary very last results.

In a reading, it's normally a merging or a taming, in all likelihood bringing together factors you already ought to combine in a latest manner. One plus four equals 5, a chaotic quantity that brings project and every now and then hassle. Temperance gives with that chaos via using the use of rearranging and balancing its additives. Reversed, Temperance can constitute the need to recall some factor in a cutting-edge day slight. So some of the gambling playing cards are approximately balance. So a good buy of our lives are approximately seeking it.

The Devil, Major Arcana Card #15

Evil. Corruption. The laden, simplistic phrases used for this card are also extremely subjective. What is evil? It relies upon really for your ideals, your manner of life, your indoctrination, your enjoy, your observations, your self. Everybody has their demons. Everybody receives trapped with the resource of them, or in them, and has to from time to time combat, or balance, their manner out. It might also moreover moreover contain one of a kind people or only your self.

That's what's depicted on this card. Beings are chained or held in location, overseen with the aid of a concept of evil that may be very real or may additionally moreover only appear actual. The Devil card often resembles the Lovers card, besides that the pair aren't free; they are certain. This card is also a six (one plus five), just like the Lovers, so it suggests a desire. My favored Devil card is Joanna Powell Colbert's remarkable Bindweed within the Gaian Tarot. The decide is held via way of manner of entangled weeds, trying not to pay attention; in despair, in desperation. To get loose, they need to choose to locate their ears and destroy the weeds.

In a reading, the maximum common interpretation elements to something chains us: addiction, obsession, oppression, and every so often clinging to errors, illusions, mistakes, and some aspect can harm you. Reversed, it often approach liberation, breaking free from barriers.

THE TOWER.

The Tower, Major Arcana Card #16

Sudden alternate, upheaval, reversal, destruction. All the ones interpretations make many human beings fear the Tower card. Those subjects can recommend cataclysm or catastrophe – and it's proper, as is often cited, that the image on many Tower gambling cards look plenty like September 11th, 2001, in New York City.

But those identical phrases, unexpected change and upheaval, can also suggest a flash of notion, a liberation, or overthrowing a lousy scenario. Destruction can as with out problems cease a few difficulty that maintains us from happiness, enlightenment, or concept. Lightning illuminates your environment, even as it startles you. It is jarring, no doubt about it, however it's colorful and revealing.

We communicate about the inspiration bringing a spark of idea, about the thunderbolt that offers us an "aha" 2d of revelation or epiphany, approximately Cupid's arrow that slams us into the divine insanity of love. They are all the Tower, too! Irrevocable change that happens now and again drives us to beautiful levels of reputation and creativity.

In a analyzing, the Tower indicators surprising, jarring exchange for specific or sick. Which course it's going is based upon on the playing gambling playing cards surrounding it, and often, you may see the trajectory. For example, are you popping out of an area of suspension or stagnation? If so, the Tower can also nicely imply liberation. This card is a seven, a training for movement. What is the plan that this sudden change well-knownshows? Reversed, the Tower speaks of lesser exchange –extra an "emptying out" than an explosion – or of a stifled launch, something no longer without a doubt determined out.

The Star, Major Arcana Card #17

The Star of Hope. The clean after the rain, the peace after the hurricane of the Tower, the uplifting breath of the river or the ocean. This card resembles Temperance in lots of decks, however right proper here, stability isn't sought with the aid of pouring the waters of existence from side to side. Balance is already accomplished. The Star pouring out the waters into the earth and the universe indicators restoration, rest, openness, connection – preserving now not some thing once more. The amount 8 (one plus seven) is motion, those recovery, soothing energies pouring forth, coming to you or from you.

In a analyzing, we typically see this card as Hope, as a time to polish brightly, to go with the waft of strength and acquire matters. It shows healing and regeneration, often every mentally and physical. The reversed card can show that there's a trouble with the manner you view the course ahead, the way you notice yourself in phrases of self-love, frame picture, or confidence. You need to be the well-known character of your very private adventure to offer and get preserve of and generate preference.

THE MOON.

The Moon, Major Arcana Card #18

The Moon taps into our intuition, into subtlety, sensitivity, and mystery, bestowing profound truths. She hangs in opposition to the darkish and shows the cycle of existence, descent and pass returned, each month within the solar's every yr cycle. The Moon is oblique, reflecting, and malleable, similar to the unconscious mind. The Sun is linear, tremendous, and based, like proper judgment and attention. Juliet's "inconstant moon" is constant best in the change that shows all matters in nature. Everything waxes and wanes. Energy grows and recedes, tides go along with the drift and ebb, light brightens and dims. Cycles are time-commemorated.

Some older Tarot traditions have a propensity to see the moon because of the reality the using pressure of madness – lunacy and every now and then violence, bathed in reflected as opposed to direct moderate. Just ask the emergency room dispatcher. Changing attitudes have refocused the reader's eye to encompass even older traditions – the moon's apparent courting to girls, to fertility, to blood ties.

So, in a studying, the Moon represents masses of things that from time to time seem contradictory, but they're definitely not: Humanity's courting to the wild and the cycles of nature, revelations, intuition, dreaming, the artist's muse, and psychic development; or lunacy, half- truths, and clandestine ravings. It's all associated, isn't it, and a rely of diploma?

The Sun, Major Arcana Card #19

Nothing is hidden inside the Sun card. We float from the contemplated mild of the moon to what it's far reflecting! It is exquisite daylight hours, midday, summer season solstice, the height of mild, the noon of the year. Most readers see the Moon as inward going thru, reflective, intuitive, and quiet. The Sun is exuberant, first-rate, satisfied, and conscious. The brightness affords clarity.

In some decks with figures dancing inside the sunshine, we see opposites coming together. In decks with one figure, we simply see happiness and pleasure.

That's what the card technique in a reading. It's a moment of pleasure, achievement, unique fitness (or recuperation), and happiness. The card's large variety, nineteen, brings us returned to the simplicity of that feeling. Nine plus 10 and that reduces to a one. In the Major Arcana, ten is the Wheel of Fortune and one is the Magician. It all speaks of excessive energy, modern cycles, and self belief. Reversed, the strength is weakened, however I don't think the huge juju of this card can be reduced to a few component bad. My recommendation should typically be to crank up the first-rate power that's observed on this card. Enjoy that day within the sunshine!

JUDGEMENT.

Judgement, Major Arcana Card #20

Judgement. Now, right here is each other card that places masses of humans on place. Sounds ominous, no? But this card is nearly typically approximately effective exchange, a revised factor of view, revelation and expertise – its different names include Awakening and Liberation.

The fear thing comes from an affiliation with the idea of punishment on the give up of the world or punishment at the give up of life. If you study the cardboard, despite the fact that, even within the oldest decks, no person is being punished or despatched away. The figures in this image are waking up, greeted thru better beings, and it's far nearly commonly snug.

There's a sense to this card that alternate has already took place. So, I've constantly idea of it as a waking up of attention due to the fact you have worked thru a adventure and decided some thing. When you awaken, you claim what you've continually identified unconsciously, that you have free will and may pick out your destiny course. There's no punishment in attempting once more. Older interpretations of this card encompass "very last willpower of a rely" and "divine interest." So, the Judgement card links yet again to the Justice card. Reap what you sow, recognize it, and make a sparkling start. Great card, huh? Reversed, it factors out denial, doubt, fear, rejection of possibility, enlightenment, or reward.

THE WORLD.

The World, Major Arcana Card #21

The fruits of the Fool's adventure via the Major Arcana is the picture of the World.

Everything and all. Fulfillment. A surely satisfied dancer appears in this card, free within the universe, wreathed in creation. This is the depiction of completely decided out lifestyles, transcendence. The wand that the figure holds harkens again to the Magician and, wherein there are wands in some decks, to the pillars of dark and moderate behind the High Priestess. The massive type of the card, twenty-one, combines the numbers of those playing cards as properly, and it makes three, the variety of recent creation.

In a reading, the World elements to a desired cease result, a step forward, an assimilation of statistics, an records of sports, a wholeness. Reversed, it can recommend stagnation and being stuck, a postpone to the fruition of a device or journey.

This is a tremendous card to throw in a studying. You realise in that you are; in the intervening time of popularity or of transferring the very last limitations for a remaining step. The World is yours.

Chapter 2: THE MINOR ARCANA

The Suits

Now that we've cited the massive energies of the Major Arcana, we're going to start our improvement through the Minor Arcana, the numbered and Court playing playing cards of the four suits. Let's begin with the suits themselves.

Just like in a modern-day deck of gambling gambling cards, there are four suits.

Pentacles or Coins correspond with diamonds and are aligned with the energies of Earth. This is the bottom, slowest vibration, and it offers with the bodily, cloth international. Think about in which you stay, what you very very very own, your body and health, and your bodily environment.

Cups correspond with hearts and are aligned with the energies of Water. This vibration gives with emotions and the way you perceive and positioned your emotions out into the arena and have interaction with specific human beings's feelings. Here you think about love and hate, harmony and struggle, forgiveness and guilt. You get the concept.

Swords correspond with spades and are aligned with the energies of air. Swords via the air – whoosh! See how the vibrations have end up higher and faster? Air is all approximately thoughts and concept – how we talk, the manner you undergo in thoughts subjects and frame them to yourself and to others. Think breath and speech.

Wands (or staves) correspond with clubs, and this is the very first-class, fastest vibration, aligning with Fire. I continually remember flaming torches. Fire is passion, creativity, the spark that makes you who you're – Fire of the Spirit.

The Numbered Cards

ACE of PENTACLES

ACE of CUPS.

The Aces

The Ace represents what is given, important, singular, foundational – a present of the spirit and the in shape in its purest shape. Aces are the stepping stone for the journey through the wholesome and supply start to all that comes after. They correspond to the Major Arcana Magician, who works with all of the elements – the given – to hold exchange to the location through their will.

The Ace of Earth/Pentacles/Coins aligns with the bodily world round us. This gift is prosperity, fulfillment. It encompasses places which you live and topics that you personal in addition for your physical nicely being.

The Ace of Water/Cups aligns with feelings. This is the present of healing, love, on the same time beneficial relationships, modern-day flow, and emotional nourishment.

The Ace of Air/Swords aligns with mind, conversation, and idea. This present is the assimilation of expertise, intellectual understanding, and readability of expression. Swords are commonly depicted as double edged – get too a long way into your head and you'll weigh down and stall your self speedy.

The Ace of Fire/Wands aligns with spirit, passion, and creativity. There is a gift of strength, enthusiasm, happiness, and optimism in this torch being passed to you.]

The Twos

Two represents stability and warfare. You can't have of some detail with out each – and that's what drama is made from! Conflict is continuously trying to remedy itself into balance with a becoming a member of or a preference. When it does, something new is born, and you circulate on via the numbered gambling cards. The High Priestess is #2 within the Major Arcana, and you may see the warfare/balance dynamic as she sits between the pillars of dark and slight, balancing them with intuition and perception.

The #2 of Pentacles aligns with Earth and the bodily worldwide. It's what we enjoy with our senses: darkish and mild, artwork and relaxation, movement and stillness, heat and cold, fitness and physical misery, loud and quiet, loads and want. You're juggling sports within the bodily, attempting to find stability.

The #2 of Cups/Water aligns with emotion. This card often suggests a pair pledging love with an exchange of emotion/water. You can, of direction, recognize the Beloved in lots of techniques, not actually romantically, and also you in no way suppose gender in the Tarot, most effective energies. Devotion, compassion, annoying, and know-how are available in plenty of paperwork, in masses of settings, and the product can be anything that is meaningful to you.

The #2 of Swords/Air is ready balancing the intellect, likely with stillness that incorporates quiet, listening, meditating, and framing - a monologue. It moreover indicates speak, - manner (or more) verbal exchange, a melding, aligning, and mixing of thoughts.

The #2 of Wands/Fire aligns with Spirit, creativity, and ardour. There is a desire being made, so there's warfare and a connection out into the sector. The 2d is resolved in one manner or any other, and I suspect it's going to probable be fiery.

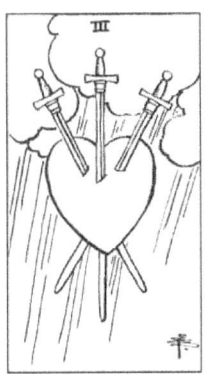

The Threes

Threes are constantly about a advent, a flowering generated from the electricity of the in shape, frequently as a part of a hard and fast dynamic. They are associated with the Empress, #three in the Major Arcana, who represents abundance, fertility, manifestation, and boom. Threes are approximately a few issue being born out of including each distinct to the stability of the two. Baby makes 3 – and "toddler" may be some thing that's being created - a task, a journey, a product, some thing is crucial in your recognition right now. In various decks, the outcomes variety throughout unique kinds of photographs, manifestation and expression.

The #three of Pentacles/Earth (or Coins in loads of decks), aligns with the bodily global. It indicates masterful paintings, developing a few factor that people admire.

The #three of Cups/Water aligns with emotions. It suggests friendship, harmony, and birthday party. This is a satisfied card, and there can be birthday party.

The #3 of Swords/Air aligns with perception and communique. There are swords piercing the coronary coronary coronary heart – heartbreak. I anticipate we're looking at an overabundance of idea. The newly-born manifestation has resulted in overthinking, obsessing. You have created an excessive amount of of a few factor mind are right here; false impression, and probably miscommunication.

The #three of Wands/Fire aligns with spirit, passion, and creativity. This card brings collectively new possibilities with rootedness or grounding. You can come to an information of what innovative energy and spirit manner for you and possibly communicate or have an exquisite time it with others. A fantastic card.

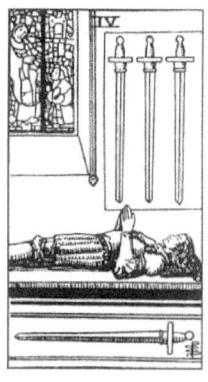

The Fours

Fours speak of shape, obstacles, basis, stewardship, and perhaps even of creating sacred place. Fours are the field for each power they represent. Throwing a 4 in a studying way that some thing is manifesting indoors a shape. You can see the rims, so you apprehend better what it looks like. The Emperor, #4 in the Major Arcana, is the ruler of the greater concrete, aware factors of existence.

The #4 of Pentacles/Earth is about possessions, cash, bodily property, and retaining all of them stable in grounded safety. They define your physical existence, and also you shield them for comfort and safety.

The #four of Cups/Water indicates a hesitancy to undertaking into that new fourth cup. Emotions round pleasure and protection are in pinnacle repute, however it's time to nourish and calm the emotional panorama with a few element new. That cup will make four, a rectangular, a sturdy shape, despite the fact that arguably lots a whole lot much less intuitive, than the three already reputation.

The #4 of Swords/Air is ready taking a damage and sinking into intellectual restfulness. Stop overthinking and rejuvenate. Unplug and recharge from a special supply. The busy mind will although be there while you get lower decrease back. This 4 is set peacefulness.

The #4 of Wands/Fire is a party of power, spirit, creativity, and passion. This card indicates us a bower or collection of loosely positioned wands, a field however not a barrier. Fire wishes air to burn, but it wants to be directed and contained, so it doesn't consume the whole thing spherical it. Light up your ardour and direct it right right into a managed burn for the consequences you need.

The Fives

Fives constitute problems, traumatic conditions, adversity, and checks via worry. I take into account them as chaos or catastrophe playing cards – throwing a wrench (or spanner, in case making a decision on) into the mechanics of our everyday lives. They are usually warnings to observe out or warnings to cope with a few component you've got got attempted to take away. Fives are hard. It's interesting that the Major Arcana card #5 is the Hierophant, the Keeper of the Keys to commonplace understanding, the trainer of a specific set of ideals or an educational tool, the authority on truth. That can be confining and the 5 possibly represents unorthodoxy or rejection of a prescribed route, inner and outward warfare, this is how we examine the Hierophant while it's reversed – and that's how masses of demanding conditions and troubles get up.

The #five of Pentacles/Earth depicts need, a disaster on a survival level within the bodily global, instead disturbing, distracting, and ingesting. You ought to create or find protection and refuge that will help you get thru the difficult instances.

The #5 of Cups/Water speaks of grief, despair, and discouragement. It points to a need for healing, an possibility to bypass the dark water, to pinnacle off the empty cups of emotion with healing that results in some issue new.

The #five of Swords/Air shows a defeat, a battle or argument that isn't going your way. The aftermath appears in lots of decks, with a lone victor and defeated opponents shifting away. Has absolutely everyone definitely obtained? Think about beliefs that couldn't be proper, approximately strategies to treatment a warfare or shield a territory with out fight, approximately the dynamics of power and warfare inside the state of affairs.

The #5 of Wands/Fire receives its electricity from conflict. This photograph indicates a chaotic warfare with staves. This card is often about managing fears and stressful situations with self-discipline, about wading in and taking part in the combat.

The Sixes

Sixes might also have us make selections. They are about identifying what is vital. The Lovers, #6 inside the Major Arcana, makes us find out the Beloved. We see reciprocity, interaction, partnership, collaboration, sharing. We moreover see unequal relationships – in plenty of decks, someone stands above and a person under in every healthful.

The #6 of Pentacles/Earth suggests a person giving coins away to balance the scales they'll be retaining. Sharing fabric items or wealth of some issue kind is the difficulty of this card, and it's continually aware giving and receiving.

The #6 of Cups/Water often includes an interpretation that acknowledges the emotion of nostalgia. The cups are status, and we see someone sharing a gift that brings happiness or beauty. This card is prepared the emotions surrounding sharing connection, wish, and warmth.

The #6 of Swords/Air shows a person poling a deliver with a hunched, struggling parent, moving across the water – to an isle? This is a card of mind and conversation, so the help supplied right proper right here is approach, love, and craft. You pick out to really take shipping of (or no longer) assist in framing and questioning.

The #6 of Wands/Fire offers us the flame of self belief, delight, and victory, shared via the large determine with the others round them. The victor/leader is surrounded via adulation. You pick out the way you have a remarkable time and percentage success and elation.

The Sevens

Sevens come up with the moments to prepare, do internal art work, and emerge as aware about the movement to go back lower again. There are factors of self-cognizance on foot through this range, in addition to making plans and putting intentions. Sevens flip inward in education and selection. The Major Arcana card #7 is the Chariot, a victory improvement or procession, a stately stillness or display a good way to sooner or later erupt into movement – however not however. Sevens flip inward in practise and choice.

The #7 of Pentacles/Earth suggests a farmer taking into consideration their crop. Of direction, that crop may be a few issue that complements their physical lifestyles or the lifestyles of the community. The next step is probably to vicinity it out into the area, but proper now may be the time to decide a manner to make the superb use of these riches.

The #7 of Cups/Water looks like possibility – all of the ones cups packed with a fable array of emotions. How will the parent use them within the global? What dream will they choose – one or many? Which manner will they glide? You can see the continuing concern depend of contemplation and planning, soaking in the feelings earlier than sharing them.

The #7 of Swords/Air suggests someone who has collected all the swords - the thoughts, communications, and thoughts – and looks to be considering a way to maintain them or use them. I've constantly notion of it as the card of the thief, in which stealth overcomes pressure, mind power triumphs over brawn, because the man or woman enjoys their cleverness.

The #7 of Wands/Fire shows a determine inside the midst of a combat using staves or wands. They must stay on top of the movement and strategize to be remarkable, persevering through the warm temperature of warfare with the warm temperature in their inner hearth, ardour, strength of will, creativity, and self-facts.

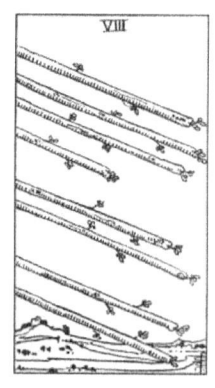

The Eights

Eights are about movement! The contemplation and check of the sevens is over and now it's time to location some element out into the arena – vision will become motion and organization turns into fact. Eights are really outward-facing. They show an detail that's transferring out into the arena, likely with some pace. Strength is the Major Arcana #8, depicting fortitude, braveness, overcoming worry, and working with staying electricity and persistence.

The #8 of Pentacles/Earth suggests an artisan turning out pentacle after pentacle, generating a flow of physical devices to reveal or offer, sharing the ones creations with others in the moment. Are they looking, learning, appreciating, shopping for?

The #eight of Cups/Water shows a person leaving the cups behind. Perhaps we're witnessing sadness or a alternate of course. Maybe the ones fantasies in the seven of cups didn't pan out. The cups are standing, no longer knocked over like inside the 5 gambling playing cards, so those cups, these feelings, can also nevertheless be possible and virtually worth including to in preference to discarding. The motion right here is away, closer to a few element not pictured – possibly a few component extra emotionally pleasing and right.

The #8 of Swords/Air indicates motion or movement hampered by using the usage of the usage of...what? There are swords, (mind and phrases and tales – endure in mind we're in the realm of mind) round this discern, but there can be a gap wherein they'll depart. The bonds are spherical their eyes and arms, however now not their legs, to be able to stand and stroll. There's a castle in the historical past, which typically represents authority, but there's no character imposing or coercing every body that we're capable of see. Is this self-imposed bondage, restricting thoughts or self-speak or beliefs? The awareness that no longer some thing in reality holds the determine is probably freeing.

The #eight of Wands/Fire is electricity in motion, flying wands, and streaming fireplace. In maximum decks, there are no people within the photograph. Spirit, creativity, ardour, notion – the additives of Tarot Fire are on the circulate, and you have the possibility to take advantage of them.

The Nines

Intensity and lots are the problem topics of the nines. Whatever your hassle be counted, a few element your query, irrespective of the perception, there's masses of it. Whether that abundance is extremely good or horrible for your intentions is predicated upon on the location of the cardboard in the format. There's furthermore the element of mastery right here – of understanding which you have finished or accrued a few aspect. Nine is the very last unmarried digit within the cycle of numbered playing playing cards and the type of months in a pregnancy, so we're looking at a achievement of the healthful. Nine is 3 instances three and portends the transport of some element, while you're close to your aim, with all of the facts, gear, and understanding, culmination of your labors, in region to get there. The Hermit, Major Arcana card #9, indicates us the seeker who is going off on my own after which returns with the lantern of enlightenment to share the statistics they've got birthed.

I constantly consider the #9 of Pentacles/Earth due to the fact the Lady within the Garden. She has finished an super life, in all likelihood via area and try, considering that this is the cardboard of the physical and fabric realm. Tarot figures are genderless, despite the fact that this feminine energy is nurturing. But the girl isn't the point – the accomplishment is. There is bounty spherical this figure, they'll be assured and prepared, and they might relaxation of their lawn of prosperity to look what will come next.

The #nine of Cups/Water includes the thoughts of emotional abundance, enjoyment, satisfaction, protection, and generosity. Maybe the cups deserted in the eights are decided or changed proper right right here and the emotional journey is fulfilled. These vessels keep what is long lasting and full-size. What will you drink from them?

The famous #nine of Swords/Air photograph is a discern sitting up in bed and covering their face even as a "ladder" of swords is going up the wall beside them. This card is ready what wakes you up at night – the fullness and misery of all the mind and recollections we inform ourselves. They are all proper right here, and you are in a place to attach them, make experience of them, and starting a new truth for yourself, laying apart fear. It is said that we feature guilt from the past and worry for the destiny. You have manipulate of ways you react inside the gift.

The #9 of Wands/Fire is an picture of perseverance, braveness, stamina, and power – it's approximately readiness. The success of Fire/Spirit is self-self assure that bestows an popularity of every possibilities and threats and the ability to stand them. There has been masses of attempt expended right proper right here and the end quit result is in sight.

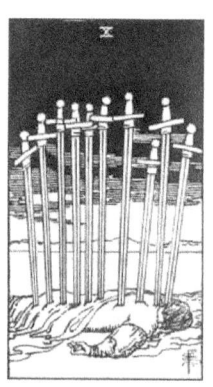

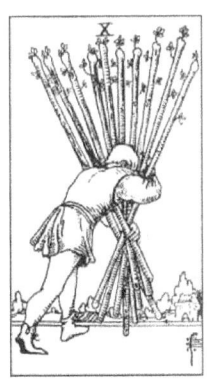

The Tens

See the tens as stop end result, extra, transition – the space is so complete that it want to now roll over into a few thing else. Remember that ten is ultimately one all over again and the start of a few other adventure, birthed in the nines. You're being given each special primary element, every other supply. The tens display us the splendor and burdens of endings and beginnings, the magic of eternal cycles. The topic is apparent within the Major Arcana card #10, the Wheel of Fortune. What ends moreover starts offevolved offevolved, what is going up need to come down, and what's down rises another time.

The #10 of Pentacles/Earth suggests the figures residing in beauty and taking element in their prosperity. We also are seeing insulation and blind privilege because of the fact the shadow aspect of the cardboard. The figures are indoors, and there may be a global out of doors, and they don't seem like collaborating in it. What will they do with all that abundance?

The #10 of Cups/Water is a celebration – happiness shared, a second of euphoria. It's one of the happiest gambling playing cards within the Tarot, to be savored – the fullness snatched in advance than it passes by means of the use of. It's constantly right, always essential, to have a extraordinary time the ones complete cups within the second.

The #10 of Swords/Air brings suffering, as a further of idea frequently does. The card is frequently study as drama, over-assessment, and hysteria. Everything isn't always amazing, however perhaps it's the belief this is most elaborate or it can be real distress, despair, or tension. There seems to be a dawning – or at the least a lighter sky – in the distance.

The #10 of Wands/Fire depicts a extremely good burden. An overabundance of passion, of fireplace, can burn proper right into a conflagration. Passion can become obsession; the author occasionally turns into a fanatic; spirit can turn out to be disassociated with the cloth. It may be a completely unique international while the hearth dies and this heavy weight of obligation has been met or has dissipated.

THE COURT CARDS

The Court Cards typically represent people or elements of your (or someone else's) persona – individual tendencies which are crucial to the issue of the analyzing. They have no gender but a number of the energies, often mixed, are what we consider as masculine or girl.

The Knight, Queen, and King correspond to the Jack, Queen, and King in gambling card decks, but in Tarot, there's a further card, the Page, the youngest and least professional of those people or components. These gambling gambling playing cards supply the equal energies for every healthy as in the numbered playing cards. Here's a recap:

Pentacles or Coins correspond with the energies of Earth, the bodily, fabric global. Think of wealth, health, and possessions.

Cups are aligned with the energies of Water. This vibration gives with emotions and the way you understand and placed your emotions out into the area and interact with top notch humans's feelings.

Swords correspond with the energies of Air, and it is all about mind and idea. Think approximately the manner you communicate, the way you consider matters, and frame them to yourself and to others. Think breath.

Wands or staves is the excellent, quickest vibration, aligning with Fire. Think of flaming torches and your passion, creativity, and the

spark that makes you who you are – Fire of
the Spirit.

Kings

The King is the ruler of the in shape. This is a masculine, organizing energy, linear, authoritative, and conscious.

In a reading, Kings in upright positions propose we're speakme approximately being in rate of the power of the healthy. You, or the individual this represents, has authority or at least great impact over how you have interplay with, order, and assemble your very very own cloth, emotional, highbrow, and non secular geographical regions. Reversed, you'll be ignoring or now not using the strength this card bestows.

QUEEN of PENTACLES

QUEEN of CUPS.

Queens

The Queen hints as properly, however through the use of the usage of nurturing and watching. I reflect onconsideration on them because of the truth the Watcher of the healthy. The electricity is more fluid, female and spiraling, intuitive and un/unconscious.

When you throw Queens in a reading, they may be telling you to take care, to nurture, to pay interest in your extra intuitive voice or to someone who cares. Watch how your bodily environment and assets are cared for. Be privy to your emotional kingdom. Decide the way you want to talk to yourself and others, the manner you intellectualize records and communicate it. Follow what lighting fixtures you up and feeds your inner being. Reversed, you can now not be the use of the subtler energies and gentler control the Queen can bring to any scenario.

KNIGHT of PENTACLES

KNIGHT of CUPS.

KNIGHT of SWORDS.

KNIGHT of WANDS.

Knights

The Knight is on a quest. They are the doer of the in shape, energetic and eager to make a few element take place.

Upright Knights are telling you to perform that. Find what needs to be determined, exchange what desires to be modified. Forge earlier. Do it – or supply out that man or woman who is supplying to apply their records to do it for you. Maybe you need to alternate or pass your bodily surroundings or deal with your fitness. Maybe you need to amplify a contemporary way of looking at thinking about or responding to a state of affairs. Maybe a revelation is there can be you gain out a take it. Reversed, you'll be moving too fast and need to gradual down, or you may no longer be taking benefit of the on the spot for movement.

PAGE of PENTACLES.

PAGE of CUPS.

PAGE of SWORDS.

Pages

The Page is the novice. They are open and ready to truely accept statistics and know-how, keen to research, organized to apprentice and/or serve. The electricity is more youthful, easy, and accepting.

Pages want to have a take a look at and are open to new reports. Are you beginning a few factor new? Is there someone who goals your education or recommendation? Are you reading a brand new situation or journeying to a cutting-edge day holiday spot? The Page is a amateur in a few way. In a reading, you can see a beginning while the page makes an appearance, or possibly a contemporary enjoy, opportunity, or popularity. Reversed, be cautious for the "been there, finished that" attitudes and the subjects that aren't serving you anymore.

Chapter 3: A Brief History Of The Tarot

Where Did The Modern Tarot Deck Originate?

A famous, enormous notion is that the tarot deck we use nowadays modified into primarily based mostly on a preferred deck of playing gambling playing cards, at the beginning created and used in the overdue 1300s, brought to Europe via exchange with Middle Eastern nations. This can be a myth, as there is no mention of some thing related to the tarot until a century later. The mysterious etymology of the phrase "tarot" is doubtful. Some speculate that it'd have originated from the Arabic phrase "taraha", meaning to location aside, or discard, even though that connection is obscure at excellent. One Swiss fact seeker believed that the phrase "tarot" first off came from the Egyptian phrases "royal road", and he posited that the tarot playing cards have been a form of divine avenue within the path of enlightenment.

While we do get our numeric device from Islamic way of lifestyles, it wasn't until the late 1400s that an alternate address present day gambling gambling playing cards, referred to as the "Triumph" gambling cards, spread like wildfire at a few degree in the Italian society. Wealthy households often commissioned artists to create costly decks of triumph gambling playing cards, a complete set of which protected the 4 fits of preferred playing playing cards in addition to the courtroom docket cards or "face gambling playing cards", but it additionally contained a further suite of snap shots gambling cards. These extra imagery cards have been created with heavy symbolism, archetypes, and iconic images, and were used as trump playing playing cards. The new triumph deck become a awesome fulfillment, and a enterprise referred to as tarocchi appropriati originated from it, loved through using manner of aristocratic society. In a pastime of tarocchi, game enthusiasts drew random gambling playing playing cards and built lyrical verses based totally mostly on what they interpreted from the card's imagery.

Tarocchi modified into later shortened to "tarot", the French phrase from which tarocchi have become tailored, and the tarot deck have become born. Draws pulled during tarocchi were nicknamed "sortes", or destinies.

French and English occultists helped the tarot deck upward thrust to reputation in the 17oos. Soon, in location of tarot being a mere parlor hobby, it started out to be identified as a valuable, effective tool of cartomancy—the workout of divining one's future through the usage of gambling cards.

In 1909, the region's most right away recognizable tarot deck, the Rider-Waite tarot, turn out to be invented. In the 70s, an creator named Stuart Kaplan published a e-book on tarot and the historic practice of tarot card analyzing became catapulted into the 20 th century.

Other Theories

There are despite the reality that questions as to where the true pictures and photograph-associated definitions came from so to traverse the wealthy societies of Italy. One principle indicates that the ideas got here from a ebook that have become misplaced even as the Egyptian library at Alexandria burned down. Trade and conquest most of the Roman Empire and Upper Egypt became a ordinary occurrence, and masses of occultists keep in mind that the tarot became one of the many treasures out of place in Alexandria's catastrophic, worldwide information-converting hearth.

Another Egypt-centric concept have become that the pics and meanings were primarily based definitely mostly on a holy ebook written in Egypt, and then brought via way of peoples who must come to be Romani tribes in Europe and Britain. The presence of triumph gambling playing playing cards predated the number one look of the Roma in European international locations, so this concept doesn't rise up as well to the others, but it's far an exciting belief.

In the overdue 17oos, a trainer and author named Jean-Baptiste Alliette wrote a ebook wherein he defined the game of "Piquet". He brought a very specific card referred to as an "Etteilla", which he substantially carried out as his nom de plume, or pen-name, created with the aid of way of the usage of reversing the letters of his very last call. The etteilla card would possibly constitute the issue or querent in a interest of piquet, and we're able to see this same exercising applied in plenty of present day-day tarot spreads, collectively with the famous Celtic go with the flow unfold.

A fascinating element is that Etteilla himself claimed to peer Egyptian symbolism inside the tarot cards. He did not however recognize that some of the ones had been Egyptian hieroglyphs, because it'd now not be till the

365 days 1799 that archeologists decided the Rosetta Stone—the crucial issue to cracking the code of historic Egyptian lettering. Etteilla believed that the tarot deck become inside the beginning designed via monks of Thoth, the Egyptian god of know-how, and then went immediately to format what is called "The Egyptian tarot". In the Egyptian tarot, we're capable of proper away understand an awful lot of the identical symbolism that exists in the Rider-Waite tarot deck, but with Etteilla's interest to Egyptian details.

Chapter 4: The Major Arcana

The Major Arcana

The twenty-two playing playing cards that make up the number one arcana of the tarot deck are the maximum recognizable and iconic of the tarot. They constitute archetypes—symbols that connect to humanity proper now, marking passages along the adventure of lifestyles. The Fool starts offevolved the route of the principle arcana, taking a courageous, honest step from his cliff to the unknown, his dog partner with the useful resource of his element, with only some property bundled in the sack he consists of over his shoulder. From this humble starting, the important arcana takes us thru barriers and miracles, pitfalls and windfalls, gaining facts along the way till we arrive on the World—our very last destination.

When you begin to learn how to study tarot playing playing cards, you can consciousness on the foremost arcana first. When you turn out to be extra comfortable with tarot readings and introduce the minor arcana right into a choice, you'll appearance to the crucial arcana cards present as foremost existence warning signs and symptoms. When a spread well-knownshows commonly crucial arcana playing cards, it technique that excellent

adjustments are stepping into the image.

zero - The Fool

The quantity of the Fool is zero, marking each the begin of a adventure similarly to the give up, in addition to the capability of infinity. Put aside any terrible connotations you have got with the word "fool", for this card asks you to assume the incredible. The Fool invitations us to dare, to dream, and to take a bounce of religion.

Upright, the Fool marks the start of something vital. It can be a present day relationship or career bypass; it could be a commercial enterprise or a contemporary domestic. Look to the minor arcana playing cards subsequent to it for clues, or if the unfold is satisfactory critical arcana, examine how they have interaction with each distinct.

Reversed, the Fool can recommend numerous subjects: Perhaps there's hesitation or procrastination regarding a awesome exchange. Additionally, a reversed card can constitute some thing that really now came into play, so this new beginning may moreover truly be at its starting—genuinely getting started. Reversals don't need to suggest something terrible—consider the hands of a clock. A reversal can virtually suggest that a electricity has simply begun, or is set to begin short. Finally, from time to time a reversed Fool can element out which you're too focused at the triumphing to appearance the destiny that is speedy drawing close. Watch out for the cliff's element.

Keywords to bear in mind for The Fool: Beginnings, faith, braveness, positivity, a few

problem new, need.

1 - The Magician

In the Rider-Waite tarot deck, the cardboard of the Magician has an abundance of symbols to take examine of. The first component you'll observe is that he factors with one hand in the direction of the heavens, and the alternative to the ground beneath his toes. There is an arcane phrase: "As above, so below". It speaks of the steadiness some of the spirit international and the fabric global— the stableness amongst Heaven and Earth, the balance among our hopes and our plans. In this situation, the Magician is a messenger between the two planes of lifestyles, connecting the two alongside along with his information and data.

In the front of him on his desk, you could see the 4 fits of the minor arcana: The sword, the pentacle, the cup, and the wand. These symbols represent the four factors: air, earth, water, and hearth, respectively. Above the magician, we are able to see the message of the Fool's endless promise contemplated in the soaring sign for infinity.

Upright Magician: Many moments in life call for we use our strain of will to succeed; the Magician represents strength of thoughts, and beckons us to apply ours. The Magician is the primary character the Fool meets along his journey, and due to the Magician's electricity over all topics, the Fool is able to awareness his will on fulfillment and anything comes subsequent.

Reversed Magician: The opposite of strength of will is illusion. It can be easy to fall prey to our very very very own complacency. It's time for an splendid, difficult look at your lifestyles and what modifications need to be made. This isn't a bad second—it's an opportunity for extra happiness. The reversed Magician can also signify which you are coming out of a length of despair, harm, or stagnation—you are gaining your power returned and are almost equipped to break loose.

The Magician teaches us that for some factor to grow to be a fact, we ought to keep in mind it first. Keywords to preserve in mind for The Magician: Will, mastery, strength, and the ability to get up our desires.

2 – The High Priestess

Following the instance of the Magician, the card of the High Priestess has many arcane symbolisms as properly. The pillars on each side of her represent the pillars of Strength (marked via the letter B, for Boaz) and of Establishment (marked with the aid of the letter J, for Jachin), hearkening lower again to the two pillars of the Temple of Solomon. Duality is the message proper right here— mild and dark, spirit and cloth, female and masculine, yin and yang.

Like the Magician, the High Priestess exists amongst each worlds, and is a kind of messenger from one to the opposite. She is likewise, but, a mediator. The crown she wears is also visible in depictions of the goddess Isis—a powerful Egyptian mom goddess, creator of miracles and a draw near healer. Isis moreover added the artwork of magic to mankind, and the High Priestess represents dealings in magical arts.

The flow on her chest is the solar flow, and represents the relationship to the four elements of earth, air, fireplace, and water. The crescent moon represents the maiden trouble of the goddess; the pomegranates constitute the historical, crone element of the goddess. She is a triple goddess parent, making be aware about the passages of existence from start to dying.

Upright, the High Priestess may be a reminder for us to simply accept as actual with our instincts, in choice to take matters at face fee. Life is complete of mysteries, however plenty of the ones mysteries can be located out if we appearance greater closely. The High Priestess beckons us to turn our popularity inward, moreover, and to take inventory of ourselves. She can also represent a female person who holds valuable knowledge.

Reversed, the High Priestess is telling us that our question may moreover moreover want extra time to be answered, and to have persistence. You also can have found your self out of place in confusion; it's time to strive a one in all a type approach to get answers. Just consider, take the name of the game direction—use your instinct.

Keywords to don't forget for The High Priestess: Magic, secrets and strategies and

strategies, the hidden, mysteries, instinct.

3 – The Empress

In the Rider-Waite tarot deck, the photograph of the Empress straight away takes us to a summer time day: Everything is expensive and growing. She is a queen enjoyable on her throne, however she is a queen in a time of peace. Her very photo conjures abundance and fertility.

This card is marked with the photo for Venus, and the entirety about the Empress synchronizes with that. She represents fertility, love, decided out capability and benefits.

Upright, the Empress brings us messages of fertility. This can be economic, creative, or physical. We are reaping the harvest we've sown, or are very close to doing so. She also can seem whilst we've been missing in areas of self-care. She lovingly instructions us to gradual down and odor the plants and flavor the easy water of the flowing motion.

Finding an upright Empress in your tarot spread can be a real indicator of excellent fulfillment.

Reversed, the Empress also can deliver to light the reality which you've been giving an excessive amount of of your self to others. Generosity and restoration are wonderful trends, however you need to reserve some of that in your own endeavors and self. Conversely, you'll be depending an excessive amount of on different people to take care of you. Balance is crucial.

eywords to recall for The Empress: Fertility,

abundance, creativity, being pregnant, achievement, care-giving.

four – The Emperor

In the Rider-Waite deck, the Emperor sits on a throne carved with photos of the astrological sign Aries, or the Ram. The Emperor is a seasoned ruler, having used his strain of will to overcome a barren landscape. He holds his electricity overtly as indicated via the use of a scepter and a golden orb. His stern face constantly regards his empire, searching out each possibility and chance to its sanctity.

The Emperor represents all the tendencies of the masculine, because of the reality the Empress represents the girl.

Upright, the Emperor represents manage as well as mastery. This manage isn't always completed best via brute stress of will, however of approach. The Emperor represents intelligence in power, and electricity for the gain of all, now not truly for energy's sake. Having an upright Emperor card on your draw also can represent a 2nd in which you'll be referred to as to take the helm of a few element important.

Reversed, the Emperor can shed mild on a scenario in that you have didn't take control, or energy has been taken from you. This may be some factor from now not getting credit score in your art work in a mission, to problems inside the own family dynamic at domestic, to an abusive dating or toxic connection in which your personal strength is being worn-out.

A reversed Emperor card also can constitute a lapse of personal control. Study your conduct and note if any of them are terrible or drawing time far from more critical devotions.

Keywords to do not forget for The Emperor: Power, authority, power paired with know-how, power of will, foresight.

five - The Hierophant

Even despite the reality that this is the fifth card of the vital arcana, the Hierophant has often of symbolism regarding the range 3. He wears 3 robes, each of a specific coloration and he wears a triple crown. He includes a triple scepter, referred to as the "Papal Cross". The Hierophant not only represents religious, civic, and religious authority, however the vital times of triplicity in human lifestyles: The aware, subconscious, and awesome-aware states of the human mind in addition to starting, lifestyles, and dying. Like the Magician, the Hierophant factors to above and under, Heaven and Earth, and has the

strength to combine them in prayer.

The Hierophant is the masculine card to in shape the female High Priestess. He is formal faith wherein she is magic.

Upright, the Hierophant represents that that is traditional and traditional. If you draw an upright Hierophant card on your spread, its recommendation is to take the already-mounted path, in place of going outdoor the field. This card can constitute signed contracts, subjects of law, and prison marriages.

Reversed, the Hierophant asks us to question the recognition quo. We may be feeling limited through certain additives of our lives, trying to interrupt out in their restraints. Perhaps we're being referred to as to rise up for someone whose rights are being violated.

Keywords to recall for The Hierophant: Establishment, religion, law, traditions.

6 - The Lovers

The conventional card of the Lovers suggests us a scene from the Garden of Eden—we're able to see Adam and Eve, the apple tree and the serpent. This card is also associated with the zodiac sign of Gemini. In the ancient beyond, the archangel of Air, Raphael, is showering the couple with blessings.

Upright, the Lovers constitute duality and harmony. It can be showing two aspects of a state of affairs, and that after every aspects are taken into consideration, balance is feasible. The Lovers can quite openly characterize the contemporary love, but it is able to moreover remind us that inside every body are natures, and that we should honor who we're—our real selves, for the excellent effects in life. An upright Lovers card can also represent a robust bond amongst humans in a tarot studying.

Reversed, the Lovers can represent miscommunication. Gemini, in addition to the gods Mercury and Elegua (whose sacred quantity is 6) are symbolic of conversation

and information. A reversed Lovers card can suggest that you're now not listening to topics efficiently, or possibly paying attention to rumors being unfold approximately someone or state of affairs. Seek the fact.

A reversed Lovers card also can suggest a courting that's in jeopardy. Reach out to reconnect and heal damaged ties via honest communique.

Keywords to keep in mind for The Lovers: Relationships, duality, partnership, communique.

7 - The Chariot

The Chariot represents a decide of Earth and of material topics, and who's moreover blessed with the aid of divine sources. This is a lucky card of movement; the Chariot moves ahead now not handiest by way of electricity, but moreover with the useful resource of accurate fortune. He has acquired this incredible fortune thru analyzing and controlling opposing powers—symbolized at the conventional card with the aid of using the black and white sphinxes that pull the chariot.

Upright, the Chariot represents our victory over demanding conditions or limitations. We have been successful through the usage of the messages of balance, statistics, faith, and personal energy. If you haven't yet been a fulfillment, the Chariot is telling you which you quickly may be via willpower and strength of thoughts, and that you need to have order on your plans. The Chariot is the opportunity of chaotic energy.

Reversed, the Chariot reminds us to check our aggression, as it doesn't serve us nicely. We must attempt for balance and a regular thoughts. The metaphorical horses pulling your chariot are pulling in contrary directions.

Focus on your desires and map out an cheaper plan to help you to accumulate them.

Keywords to keep in mind for The Chariot:

Determination, power, manage.

eight - Strength

This card may in all likelihood appear to have a sincere that means earlier than everything, however have a look at it cautiously: There is a girl conquering a lion, but lovingly, gently. The Strength card is as masses about inner electricity as it's miles approximately outer power, as well as grace below strain.

Often in existence, the most hard element to keep is compassion. Strength asks us to contain that during whatever scenario is handy. Brute power may be easy to expose—but having both electricity and power of thoughts, kindness and stability is what makes a person truely strong.

Upright, the Strength card tells you that you have what it takes to weather the hurricane. The Strength card moreover reinforces the fact that you live calm in times of duress, a trait you need to take satisfaction in. You have compassion for others, and it suggests.

Reversed, the Strength card can be a reminder to save you throwing your weight round recklessly, and to stroll a mile in someone else's footwear. True electricity entails stability and electricity of will. Also, a reversed Strength card may additionally constitute the return of energy—bodily, in case you're recovering from an harm or infection, emotional, in case you've suffered a unhappiness or breakup, or non secular, if you've misplaced your faith in some thing and are equipped to rebuild it.

Keywords to keep in mind for Strength: Self-

manipulate, persuasion, compassion, kindness, stability.

9 – The Hermit

The range nine is said in Norse folklore, and the Hermit can be related to a tale wherein someone spent time inside the World Tree, taking into account his destiny for 9 nights. In the traditional card layout, there may be a six-pointed movie star within the Hermit's lantern, representing Solomon's interest.

The Hermit represents someone actively looking for know-how, and understanding the sacrifices that should be made a extremely good manner to gain it. He is aware of the journey in advance of him and isn't dashing to get the cease; he realizes every step is vital to his experience.

Upright, the Hermit tells us that every now and then, solitude is for the great. Perhaps you need to step again and take inventory of your existence, otherwise you need affirmation that deciding on to go decrease lower back to highschool or getting to know a modern day expertise have grow to be a clever preference. The Hermit tells us that being by myself want no longer be lonely. Self-pondered picture can obtain bountiful rewards, with persistence. The Hermit in a analyzing can also represent someone who will mentor you or percentage their experience with you in a high-quality manner.

Reversed, the Hermit cautions us that possibly now isn't a high-quality time to be isolated. Often in times of traumatic situations, boundaries, hardships, or depression, the intuition is to shy away from those who would probably help us. The reversed Hermit gently urges us to reap out for resource.

Keywords to maintain in thoughts for The Hermit: Isolation, contemplation, analyzing, soul-searching, meditation, university university college students and apprentices.

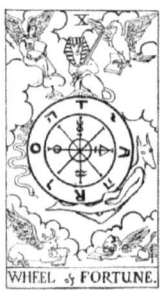

WHEEL of FORTUNE.

10 - The Wheel Of Fortune

There isn't any mistaking the symbolism of the Wheel of Fortune card. Symbols of fulfillment and correct fortune enhance it, along with the four fixed zodiac signs and symptoms and signs: Aquarius, Leo, Scorpio, and Taurus, and 4 mythical winged creatures: A bull, an eagle, a lion, and an angel. The addition of wings to the bull and lion remind us that achievement is a aggregate of perseverance and divine preference. Each being holds a financial ruin from the ancient Torah—a ebook of law and inner expertise. The photos at the Wheel of Fortune card are cyclical: The horned decide of the satan or Anubis, God of the underworld, rides the wheel upward because it turns, while the snake—image of knowledge and fabric items, rides the wheel down. This repeats again and again in a by no means-completing cycle. The sphinx, representing statistics, watches over all.

The Wheel of Fortune is a especially interesting card as its upright and reverse meanings are very comparable: Life is ready americaand downs, correct and awful. Do now not fear too much approximately the lousy, as the entirety is brief.

Upright, the Wheel of Fortune represents pinnacle accurate fortune, right fortune, and a 2d of abundance. Use it accurately because it will now not stay for all time.

Reversed, the Wheel of Fortune reminds us that every one terrible moments will skip. Our lives are in regular motion; higher days are at the horizon. Do not be proof towards exchange, because of the truth change is a crucial part of existence.

Keywords to bear in mind for The Wheel of Fortune: Luck, movement, karma, change,

evolution, increase.

eleven - Justice

Justice is a sincere card; it is frequently harassed with Judgment. Justice may be considered just like karma. The discern on the card suggests us their white shoe, indicating a divine, famous detail to it. Every motion has a final consequences and this is the message Justice is giving to us.

Upright, the Justice card tells us that we might have truely that—justice. If the difficulty emerge as wronged within the beyond, the Justice card guarantees a decision. This card additionally suggests that the alternatives we make in recent times will constantly have a result in the future, so select out correctly. Justice is sincere and balanced; this card also can suggest that the problem of the studying has correctly balanced their affairs. Additionally, this card can constitute the reality of a preserve in mind—it is able to verify some issue a card subsequent to it in a studying has said, or it may reassure you that the fact will pop out. Finally, the upright Justice card also may be a warning if the hassle of the reading has harm others.

Reversed, the Justice card may be a be-careful call that the issue of the analyzing isn't taking responsibility for their moves. It can also recommend an unfair ruling in a criminal bear in mind.

Keywords to consider for Justice: Balance, criminal topics, fairness, equality, karma,

results.

12 – The Hanged Man

In this card, the Hanged Man is showed placing the wrong manner up on what a few could in all likelihood don't forget a bypass, for others, a tree. Regardless of what he's setting from, he appears pretty at peace with it—cushty, even. The Hanged Man is not a terrible card the least bit. It's a card that represents boom, and contemplation. The Hanged Man is idea to have selected this country of short suspension, so he can get his thoughts collectively. The halo round his temples represents enlightenment. This card reminds us that now not the entirety about lifestyles is ready pushing ahead with momentum—occasionally we must prevent, breathe, and look inward earlier than taking the subsequent step on our adventure.

Not really all of us has the foresight or perception to recognize after they need to save you, however. The Hanged Man might be drawn even as the priority of the reading feels that life has all of sudden come to a halt. The reading need to be able to deliver an explanation for why, and what the hassle desires to do next. Upright, the Hanged Man asks us to pause, and feature a while for mirrored image. Many human beings attempt to fill every hour of each day with gadgets off our to-do list, and after some time, we will get burnt out. The Hanged Man fortuitously indicates us via manner of example that it's every best, and wholesome, to take a harm. He can also arrive while we're approximately to screw up—take greater time to think subjects thru before you're making an critical choice.

Reversed, the Hanged Man displays the venture's frustration approximately a effective scenario, one wherein they sense they've poured their attempt into while receiving not some thing in move back. This can be a dating, a assignment, a non-public alternate alongside side fitness or studying a ultra-cutting-edge skill. Take a have a observe the alternative playing cards within the reading to get an idea how to show matters round.

Keywords to preserve in mind for the Hanged Man: Surrender, get rid of, taking a 2nd to pause, confusion and indecision, self-reflected

image.

13 - Death

Look carefully at this card. Death is covered thru armor—he is absolute and invincible. Yet, he rides a white horse and consists of a banner of a white flower, each of which represent purity. Death is a cycle, and inevitable—death is both an ending and additionally a beginning.

Rarely does the Death card in a analyzing represent an actual, physical lack of existence; it most usually shows a remarkable exchange coming to 1's existence, and a trade from which incredible blessings will stop quit result. Death shows the end result of a period of one's life, and that it is time to move onto the following phase. For some of us, it could be hard to transport on—despite the truth that the period we're announcing goodbye to has been typically horrible, and accurate topics look ahead to for us at the horizon. Change may be uncomfortable, however it's miles a necessary part of being alive. So, paradoxically, the Death card is reminding us to stay.

Upright, Death technique transition, transformation, and exquisite exchange. These can regularly be unexpected and surprising, however relying on the opportunity cards inside the analyzing, might be sluggish and sluggish. A not unusual companion in a analyzing with Death is the Tower, in which case, the change might be unexpected, and sweeping—but at the same time because the dust settles, you'll be higher off. Death in the upright characteristic is also a advice to rid yourself of dangerous behavior.

Reversed, the Death card is gentler. You have time right now to appearance inward, and phrase if exchange in a few vicinity of your life will serve you higher and bring you more joy. Death reversed moreover represents a non-public, personal transformation—some thing that the concern of the reading goes thru internally, or behind closed doorways.

Keywords to do not forget for Death: Endings

and beginnings, new milestones in existence, top notch and surprising alternate, transformation or healing.

14 - Temperance

In this card we see an angel, flawlessly composed and calm, pouring sacred water from one cup to the following. The angel's foot is dipped into the water of a float, on the same time as the opposite hovers in the air, indicating stability.

Temperance is a mild message for us to have a have a examine our very own balance, and if it's lacking, to correct it.

When Temperance is upright in a studying, it could recommend some numerous things: It may additionally moreover furthermore constitute a person—which encompass yourself—who has mastered the artwork of stability and whose capabilities are wanted in the intervening time. It can mean that the state of affairs of the studying desires to use their calm view to evaluate a state of affairs. If the challenge is you, Temperance can be telling you which you have carried out a superb method in navigating a hard situation.

Reversed, the Temperance card may additionally moreover recommend that the problem of the reading is in hazard of losing control; they want to gradual down, take inventory, and balance the precise areas in their life or their emotions, or every.

Keywords to endure in mind for Temperance:

THE DEVIL.

Balance, calm, duality, equality.

15 – The Devil

This might be one of the most alarming gambling gambling playing cards of the maximum vital arcana to three, but what is critical is what the Devil symbolizes. In the traditional Rider-Waite deck, he is verified because the strict-faced, half of-guy, 1/2 of-goat deity Baphomet. A man and a woman, stripped of their garb, are chained to his throne to reveal that he has strength over them. In fact, they, too, activity horns—some different photo to reveal that he's converting them.

Unlike the figures in The Lovers tarot card, the figures right proper right here look sad.

Upright, the Devil suggests that you are feeling powerless approximately a few aspect. You have out of place your strength of mind, or part of your identity. You have some art work to do—find out the deliver of your imbalance. It is probably every other character taking your private power from you, or it is probably a awful dependancy which you have not began to conquer. The Devil as Baphomet factors to hedonistic indulgence in pride, and at the same time as delight is a pleasant praise of being alive, an excessive amount of indulgence can motive addiction and self-remedy on the equal time as there is emptiness in a single's existence.

Reversed, the Devil turns into a extraordinary card—it may symbolize overcoming addiction or regaining one's personal electricity. It also can represent either the begin of becoming addicted or powerless, or the start of escape from both of these items.

Keywords to take into account for The Devil: Loss of power, dependancy, low arrogance, hedonistic conduct.

16 - The Tower

The Tower is every other card that strikes fear even because it seems in a studying. It calls to mind the Tower of Babel, which modified into struck down while people exceeded their capabilities with their goals. In this context, one would likely think about the dangers of conceitedness or pleasure.

Looking deeper into this card, however, you'll be in a function to accumulate that, really as death effects in rebirth, so does destruction make manner for emblem spanking new creation. The Tower does no longer constantly imply a awful have an effect on. It is prepared terrific, sudden, sweeping trade— and change is important for boom, top fortune, and success.

Upright, the Tower can suggest a far-wanted ending to a few element that became horrible or out-lived. It also can constitute a spark of idea, or an epiphany. It also represents the surrender of a cycle—fast and complete.

Reversed, the Tower represents a refusal to trade, or being stuck in a rut. The crumbling Tower is built on unstable foundations; it can't final. Letting move of what now not serves you—or in no way served you the least bit—is healthful.

Keywords to undergo in thoughts for The Tower: Momentous trade, falsehoods

toppled, idea, epiphany.

17 - The Star

The Star is related with the zodiac sign of Aquarius, and we can see a parent of a water-bearer on this card. Eight-pointed stars surround the parent, symbolizing choice. The landscape is that of spring, wherein need returns after an extended wintry climate. The Star seeks to resume our power, and acts as a beacon to persuade us out of the darkness.

Upright, the Star seeks to remind us of the benefits we have were given in our existence. It signifies renewal, recovery, and want. It can also mean an give up to suffering. You have survived your trials and are in your way to happiness.

Reversed, the Star reflects an attitude of hopelessness and melancholy. However, we want desire in times of trouble. The reversed Star moreover asks us to dig deeper and use that reserve of power to hold going.

Keywords to bear in mind for The Star:

Renewal, refreshment, wish, religion, the stop of a tough time.

18 - The Moon

The snap shots on the Rider-Waite model of the Moon talk of stability and the dual nature of factors: There is a domesticated dog and a wolf, towers representing the forces of proper and evil, and fields divided by means of the use of the use of a flow into indicating the conscious and unconscious thoughts. The Moon is a card of mystery and instinct. It tells us to simply accept as proper with our instincts so as to navigate a landscape that is not virtually visible beneath the uncommon slight of the moon.

Upright, the Moon beckons us to face our fears and have a take a look at our way of searching at a state of affairs—are we being fooled through pointers or illusions? Something you located is real can be a lie. Dig deeper. Additionally, if you have been looking for a time to do so or make an essential selection, the Moon card in a studying can be advising you to wait till matters are clearer.

Reversed, the Moon can reflect anxiety within the assignment of a studying. A reversed Moon also can be a pleasing signal that a duration of darkness or confusion is in the long run coming to an save you.

Keywords to keep in mind for The Moon: Mystery, obstruction, primal instincts, limited

sight.

19 - The Sun

The Sun is one of the maximum first-rate gambling cards of the critical arcana. It depicts an unclothed toddler the use of a white horse of purity, basking within the recovery rays of the solar. A wall of sunflowers rises up in the distance, indicating the peak of summer season.

Upright, the Sun represents accurate fortune and abundance, similarly to a pleasant "certain" to a question asked inside the studying. It is a customary "thumbs-up" that subjects are going as they ought to be, and that they are going nicely. The Sun card moreover speaks for the reality which you are seeing subjects actually, and that you will be in a position to percentage your particular fortune with others.

Reversed, the Sun warns of focusing an excessive amount of at the horrific, or factors to some element particular this is preventing your achievement. Alternatively, a reversed Sun card can propose being overly confident approximately some thing. Take time to examine the state of affairs and find out any weaknesses or flaws that can be stepped forward upon.

Keywords to take into account for The Sun: Abundance, correct success, everyday pick out, generosity.

20 - Judgment

Gabriel the archangel sounds the trumpet calling the useless to upward push from their graves at the Judgment card. A wall of water rises within the historical beyond, poised to sweep the Earth smooth. Judgment reminds us that the results of our choices are inevitable, however as quickly as its have an effect on has exceeded, we're capable of begin anew. The Judgment card is associated with Pluto and the afterlife, and is set up to the card of Death.

Upright, the Judgment card calls for us to assess ourselves or a scenario. It is time to region apart ego and use focused, independent evaluation to move earlier. Upright Judgment also can mirror an awakening indoors yourself or the project of the reading.

Reversed, the Judgment card presentations judging oneself or each distinct too harshly. Judgment is independent, and so have to we be at the identical time as assessing a situation or an man or woman. Avoid rumination—obsessing on beyond errors—and alternatively, select out objectivity even as self-reflecting. A sentence that is too harsh is an unjust sentence.

Keywords to recall for Judgment: Analysis, awakening, revelation, transferring beforehand from an area or situation.

21 - The World

The World is a terrific card to have turn up in a reading. It talents a benevolent, triumphant discern floating towards a blue sky, retaining batons. The parent is surrounded by way of the 4 divine creatures: An angel, an eagle, a bull, and a lion, representing Aquarius, Scorpio, Taurus and Leo, respectively, and staining the 4 corners of the universe. The World card is prepared ideal stability and concord, and pinnacles of achievement.

Upright, the World stands for enlightenment, accomplishment, and completion. You have reached the stop of an technology or length of increase, trials, or gaining knowledge of, and you've got were given risen up to a better level.

Reversed, the World can point to a country of feeling incomplete. Perhaps the state of affairs of the studying has attained and purchased many things, but the ones gadgets have not succeeded in making them happy. Re-examine your values and dreams.

Keywords to don't forget for The World: Success, of entirety, fulfillment, balance.

Chapter 5: The Minor Arcana

The Minor Arcana

The fifty six playing cards of the tarot's minor arcana are related the fits and figures of a famous deck of gambling gambling cards used in recent times. The playing cards of the minor arcana are there to add more that means and nuance to the formidable statements made through any essential arcana playing playing playing cards in a studying. Minor arcana playing cards can thing to a selected man or woman, a particular location within the trouble's lifestyles, or the emotions linked to the records of the reading. While maximum important arcana gambling playing cards can communicate of a large, prolonged-lasting have an effect on, minor arcana playing playing cards display us impacts which is probably short.

The Suit of Cups, connected with the usual gambling cards' hearts match, represents emotions and connections. It is established with the element of Water.

The Suit of Swords, related with the standard playing playing playing cards' spades in shape, represents thoughts, motion, and concept. It is associated with the detail of Air.

The Suit of Pentacles, related with the same old gambling playing playing cards' diamonds in form, represents wealth, paintings, and subjects of the material plane. It is related to the detail of Earth.

The Suit of Wands, associated with the same old playing cards' clubs healthful, represents energy, suggestion, creativity and evolution. It is associated with the detail of Fire.

It is simple to apply a deck of playing cards for a minor arcana tarot studying—use the kind of analyzing to have a have a study everyday topics. If a reading consists of generally minor arcana, then the task of the reading is being requested to check their each day existence.

The Suit of Cups

The Ace Of Cups

A hand holds a golden chalice from which 5 streams glide. The streams constitute our five senses. When you purchased the ace of cups in a analyzing, it's miles beckoning you to partake in happiness. Perhaps you've got were given were given been keeping returned from experiencing sturdy feelings. The ace of cups needs you to permit cross, and experience this second for your existence to the fullest.

Upright: An possibility for happiness awaits you if you're formidable enough to jump ahead. A duration of pain or trauma is over, and you'll be healed. Alternatively, your creativity is at an all-time immoderate—make the brilliant use of it for a achievement results.

Reversed: Your emotions are being taken as a right or wasted. The waters in the cup are pouring out into the sea right here, leaving the cup empty. Someone may be taking you for granted or taking gain of you. Perhaps you're running too difficult for too little outcomes. The ace of cups reversed can also advocate which you are neglecting your private emotional care, or need to feed your innovative aspect if it's been

omitted.

The Two Of Cups

The of cups is a specifically correct sign to reveal up in a reading concerning love and relationships. It is also auspicious in a analyzing approximately contracts, organization partnerships and cash. Two figures stand in a rite, changing goblets. The picture of the caduceus represents the power of the cosmos, trade and alternate, and an honorable code of behavior. A chimera presides over the occasion, symbolizing the detail of hearth. The of cups is a card of concord.

Upright: A fortunate partnership, relationship, or contractual agreement in its early levels. Mutual recognize. Balance and fairness. The capacity for exceptional matters within the future.

Reversed: Imbalance amongst   activities. Resentment, nitpicking, or abuse of energy.

The of cups reversed factors out a need for someone to talk up and try to bridge the distance, and make subjects right another time.

The Three Of Cups

The three of cups suggests three girls, their

heads adorned with wreaths, toasting every different and dancing in a circle. This card suggests a time for celebration—the imminent together of kindred spirits, pals, or circle of relatives, and a reunion of those who have been apart. It also can show the effect of the goddess, as triple goddess: Maiden, mother, crone. It shows right instances and bountiful days. The 3 of cups can also factor to a a fulfillment collaboration in enterprise agency or cutting-edge endeavors.

Upright: Joyful times, reunion, circle of relatives, collaborative work primarily based on satisfaction or ardour for the sector. If you have got been going it by myself for a while, the 3 of cups reminds you to obtain out and connect to your human beings once more, due to the fact connection and collaboration frequently brings out the exquisite in us. You have been a hermit for a while, socially; this card encourages you to get out amongst people all over again, and you will discover happiness there.

Reversed: Social burn-out, the want to withdraw, or recuperation from overindulgence. There are instances to be with different human beings and there are instances to be via one's self: The three of cups reversed shows that you want some by myself time to consciousness to your

responsibilities and dreams, or simply to clean your head.

The Four Of Cups

The 4 of cups indicates a person seated towards a tree, his hands folded stubbornly. Though there are three whole cups inside the front of him, and a paranormal entity offers him a fourth from mid-air, he stays unimpressed.

The 4 of cups seems to expose us that we are not identifying gratitude for the treasures that we have were given. We may be more centered on losses, or subjects no longer but conceivable, and so our accomplishments and real abundance flow into left out.

Alternatively, the four of cups can also additionally seem to verify that on the identical time as there can be opportunities and gives at the table, we are not but satisfied that any of those are the "right match". Look at this card to inspire you to stick on your weapons, and now not act until the right away is ideal for you. Perhaps you are not but organized to take some trouble on, however with time and revel in, you'll be. The guy inside the card isn't outright rejecting the cups supplied to him—he's sincerely geared up. Yet some special way of searching on the upright 4 of cups is someone who can't see the best possibilities before them. Take into interest which state of affairs is because it must be mirroring your personal.

Upright: Untapped sources, waiting to act, possibilities for abundance and new connections positioned on hold.

Reversed: A length of looking inward. An introverted character who would as an opportunity spend time thru themselves. Ignoring matters that you are feeling too exhausted to address proper now. Procrastination.

The Five Of Cups

In this card, a mournful discern carrying a black cloak hides their face. Three chalices lay empty and spilled at the floor, however to remain upright. The river acting as a barrier

many of the man or woman and the house

within the distance represents sturdy emotions. This is a card of loss, of being overwhelmed by way of manner of manner of disappointment. The character in the card is immobilized and doesn't see that there are despite the fact that pinnacle topics of their lifestyles.

Spilled cups on this context represent omitted or wasted possibilities. Being stored from one's domestic shows some thing scary event that's befell has left the concern of the reading ungrounded. They want to regroup and stabilize, and open their eyes to the pleasure that also exists inside the worldwide, and of their life.

Upright: Off middle, self-pity, grief, mourning the shortage of an opportunity, courting, aid, or individual. The want for forgiveness—either of your self or of someone else.

Reversed: Blaming yourself harshly for a mistake. The need to reconcile with the fact that you can't remake the past, and which

you need to transport in advance.

The Six Of Cups

An idyllic scene is depicted displaying one infant giving the prevailing of a cup of blossoms to any other, in the courtyard of a sunny citadel. The six of cups takes us again to our early life. It is full of nostalgia for happier, less complicated times.

This card moreover symbolizes concord and happy unions. It can appear if you have misplaced your inner little one, and on the identical time as your lifestyles needs more a laugh and interesting sports activities sports.

Upright: The joys of early reminiscences, nostalgia, innocence, platonic love.

Reversed: Being stuck inside the beyond, the dearth of joy in one's every day sports. The six of cups can also display up in a reading if you have been forgiven thru someone, while you your self have forgiven someone, or while you

want forgiveness for your self or a person else.

The Seven Of Cups

The seven of cups is the card of delusion and of desires. Seven cups contain remarkable treasures or wonders to an astonished decide. This cup appears even as we are targeted on our dreams, or whilst remarkable possibilities are being offered to us now or within the near destiny.

This card also represents wishful wondering. It is vital to have dreams and goals, however it's additionally important to have a robust, grounded plan on a way to acquire them. Dreaming can remarkable get us up to now— we want motion to peer our goals come to lifestyles.

This card may additionally endorse confusion within the face of too many gives. Take time to assess every one wisely.

Upright: Appealing options, opportunities, wishful questioning, having a pipe dream, phantasm, delusion.

Reversed: A feeling of being beaten, an excessive amount of of a outstanding element, pragmatism, re-comparing values.

The Eight Of Cups

Beneath the slight of a dozing moon, a person begins offevolved a voyage right right into a mysterious panorama, leaving in the back of his collection of golden cups. The eight of cups represents a shift in wondering—leaving inside the decrease back of the old requirements for a cutting-edge adventure of discovery. The eight of cups can be symbolic of an internal non secular adventure, an actual shifting of residence or profession, or surely re-comparing what is crucial to us. It often shows a shifting an extended manner from a former aim of fabric acquisition, to some factor greater emotionally, spiritually, or intellectually enjoyable.

Upright: Change, transition, adulthood. Seeking solutions. A shift of significance positioned from the cloth to the non secular. Returning to training. The search for a higher motive.

Reversed: Uncertainty and confusion. Being dissatisfied, however no longer understanding why or what to do approximately it.

The Nine Of Cups

In this card, we see a person who is finished and certainly pleased with himself. His tremendous series of cups stands within the back of him, ordered neatly and displayed for all to appearance. The nine of cups is a card of achievement, accomplishment, and the delight that results from each.

As one of the higher-numbered cups on this suite, the 9 of cups speaks of survival, and popping out in advance after a journey of u.S.And downs. Every suite—cups, swords, pentacles, and wands—further to the principle arcana symbolizes a adventure while checked out as an entire message. The nine of cups tells us that we've got had been given survived our ordeals and trials, triumphantly.

Upright: A wonderful financial america, accolades, wholesome satisfaction, fulfillment, recovery, victory.

Reversed: Feeling unfulfilled, empty satisfaction, a meaningless accomplishment and the want to discover what you actually

need in existence.

The Ten Of Cups

A surely celebratory card, the 10 of cups shows a happy couple admiring a rainbow arching over their heads, on the same time as innocent youngsters play around them. Ten cups hover over the rainbow, banner-like, and a non violent historical beyond of a geographical place in the summer season sums up this image of entirety, togetherness, and pleasure.

The ten of cups is a robust indication that lousy times or troubles are over, and happiness is on its way, if it's not right here already.

When this card seems, dreams are being fulfilled, and the difficulty of the analyzing is enjoying or speedy will enjoy an abundant, satisfied existence.

Upright: Union, marriage, a satisfied dating, concord, very last contact, a very satisfied existence.

Reversed: What modified into idea to be an remarkable union or lifestyles became based on illusions. A reassessment of values and goals is desperately desired. What modified into as quickly as a happy relationship is stricken by loss of communique—probably one associate has grown in a course that has them drifting some distance from the alternative. Loving communication is needed.

The Page Of Cups

The internet page of cups is a specially fanciful, if now not whimsical, card. A theatrical decide holds a cup, gazing a paranormal fish that appears to need to engage him in conversation. This card is a piece similar to the joker card—it suggests some element surprising, but not usually terrible; in truth, it is able to be an sudden

boon.

The internet web page of cups seems while there are possibilities to be had to you, however pleasant if you use your instinct. You need to count on outside the world and anticipate the sudden. Additionally, if you have been knowledgeable to save you chasing a dream due to the reality a person else has judged that dream ridiculous, the internet page of cups is proper proper right here to remind you that simplest you could select how important your goals are. Resist others' grievance and hold on together with your plans; in fact, paintings even extra hard to reap your dreams, irrespective of how remarkable they might appear in your critics.

Upright: Persistence, the surprising, imagination, goals granted.

Reversed: Pessimism, bowing to strain from others, being too mired in way of existence,

the need to carve out one's very very own direction.

The Knight Of Cups

The discern pictured within the Knight of Cups card bears a cup stuffed alongside together with his very personal emotions. He is giving away from his coronary heart. Wings enhance him, symbols of creativity and creativeness. He is not charging beforehand on his horse; he actions in the direction of that whom he admires with poise and charm.

In the Rider-Waite deck, the records of this card isn't always lush, however the knight guarantees rejuvenation. When this card appears, you have were given got a want to create, or to move spherical within the global and admire its herbal beauty.

Upright: Falling in love or love supplied, romance, a modern venture in order to be restorative, a rejuvenation of price variety. You live lifestyles stimulated thru the beauty round you in all things. Making a choice based on emotions.

Reversed: Constant having a pipe dream, refusal to accomplish that, jealousy, disillusionment, melancholy.

The Queen Of Cups

The nice card on this suite that shows a closed cup, the Queen of Cups symbolizes emotions rooted within the spirit and soul. She is as deep as the sea itself, and is not brief to reveal her secrets. Her wealth of compassion is boundless. She is in contact along facet her emotions but they do no longer weigh down her, as symbolized via her toes now not touching the sea's waters, but resting on colorful stones.

Upright: Giving or receiving compassion, a caring man or woman, the use of one's instinct, going with existence's herbal go together with the go together with the flow.

Reversed: Swimming upstream, a closed coronary heart, co-dependency, hidden emotions, the need for self-care.

KING of CUPS.

The King Of Cups

In this card, we see a serene, affected individual, and nicely-controlled guy who has mastered the feelings symbolized in his clothing and surroundings. As we've visible in distinct water gambling cards, the king has one foot pointed towards the sea that surrounds his throne, indicating a steady stability most of the material international and the non secular international, and the conscious and unconscious mind.

The King of Cups card contains excellent have an impact on; it's miles a strongly excessive first-class signal that you may have an outstanding pal in you endeavors, creatively, concerning abundance, and from someone captivated with assisting others. It additionally symbolizes the truth that you have mastered your emotions. They now not control you, and you take element in the advantages of living a peaceful, balanced existence.

Upright: Abundance, creativity, mastery over emotions.

Reversed: Chaotic feelings, the want for recuperation, letting your coronary coronary heart rule your head.

The Suit Of Swords

The Ace Of Swords

The ace of swords card maximum commonly indicates an highbrow bounce forward of some type. It implies mastery of the thoughts, and a decisive motion based totally on research or considerate planning. It additionally represents the ambition of the state of affairs of the studying.

Upright: The blade of a sword can lessen thru many things, on the aspect of whatever obscuring the reality. This card often seems whilst reality is ready to be placed. Upright ace of swords moreover way concept, a breakthrough moment, or an prolonged-awaited exchange sooner or later coming to fruition. You might also additionally experience a alternate of viewpoints which can motive accomplishments and greater opportunities.

Reversed: This model of the ace of swords symbolizes confusion and chaos. It's a negative time to make crucial selections or options.

The Two Of Swords

In this card, we see a woman blindfolded, shielding swords which might be in addition balanced. The two of swords symbolizes

confusion—we must make a preference, but at this component in time, it's impossible to determine which one is the proper choice. Take word of the moon in the ancient beyond. This offers to the trouble, as the moon is shrouded in mystery and phantasm.

Upright: The want for fact and additional facts. If the analyzing is prepared art work or industrial organisation, do now not act until you get maintain of greater facts. You may be looking for a reply from a brand new system, purchaser, boss, or employee, but don't mistake the delayed response as an answer. Have staying electricity and the answer will come. Alternatively, the upright of swords can thing to the fact that a person is refusing to stand the reality. By ignoring a trouble, it's going to no longer leave.

Reversed: Two forces are in opposition, and neither may want to make a float. Stalemate.

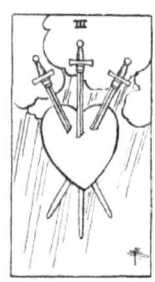

The Three Of Swords

Several iconic gambling playing cards of the tarot deck have the power to shake the reader—that is most certainly one in all them. The three of swords suggests a coronary heart pierced via three blades, set inside the route of a turbulent sky. Lashing rain is launched thru clouds. The feeling expressed with the aid of this card is felt proper now—the area we symbolically preserve to preserve our warmth, love, and humanity is being attacked.

Upright: Rejection, betrayal, abandonment, unexpected loss. Remember that that may be a swords card, and the sword represents the element of air, and the mind. Rely in your mind to help you get via the ones troubling subjects of the coronary heart.

Reversed: The symbolism and message of this card is assuaged fairly in reversal, but now not a whole lot. It can suggest that a loss, deliver of grief, or betrayal modified into inside the close to beyond, and that we're walking on restoration from it, although wounds are

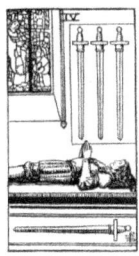

although fairly clean.

The Four of Swords

Again, we're reminded that the tarot playing playing cards tell a tale and comply with a linear course. Here a carved discern atop a crypt lies in repose, hands clasped in slight prayer. The three swords that pierced the coronary heart in the preceding card are displayed at the wall. In the stained-glass window beyond is a satisfied scene of domestic and own family, possibly relaying that, after the pain, the victim of the swords has found peace regardless of the whole thing.

Upright: This card indicates a time of relaxation, or retreat. It may be involuntary, because the problem may be exhausted or overwhelmed via the disturbing even that during truth befell. Or, it could be what the unfold is recommending—prevent now and stop combating, or you can burn yourself out. Some wounds want extra time to heal.

Reversed: You or the problem of the analyzing is refusing to back off, and this is endangering yourselves. You are strongly advised to take a hiatus of some kind.

The coronary heart need to be healed, for

without it, we definitely can not stay.

The Five Of Swords

The 5 of swords depicts what can only be defined because the "triumphing equal of a sore loser". A young determine gloats over the victory of others he has bested in warfare. An conceited smile on his face, he has claimed extra swords than he can also even deliver.

This card makes it very easy that you or someone else has chosen winning over harmony.

Upright: While you may think which you have emerged from a warfare excessive best, in fact you've got managed to make matters worse. Your recognition and connections can also additionally furthermore were compromised with the resource of your aggression and gloating. If you act on this and try to repair the damage that's been completed with some humility and honest conversation, you will be capable of salvage the state of affairs and your very own recognition, because the wounds are although quite sparkling.

Reversed: You or someone else has already decided out that the conflict modified proper right into a mistake. Now they're biding their time, seeking out the dust to settle. It's

despite the fact that not too past due to repair fences.

The Six Of Swords

In this card we see a female and toddler being ferried away. With their backs to us and their cloaks overlaying their faces, we gain the have an effect on that they may be leaving a few element within the again of and transferring inside the path of a new future. The six of swords seems at the same time as some element that has us, added us ache, or no longer serves us is being left within the once more of, with a promise of a better destiny beforehand. The swords inside the boat represent the fact that we however endure scars from beyond sports, or that we are able to usually carry the memories of them.

Upright: Transition, but no longer in reality certainly one of desire. Letting flow into, as it's the best way to steady a happier future. The slow, grueling device of recuperation.

Reversed: Trouble with moving on. Either you're experiencing stressful situations and boundaries which might be keeping you stuck in your modern scenario, or you may't appear to get your head and your coronary coronary heart out of the beyond. You may additionally resent the reality that you need to skip on.

The Seven Of Swords

The seven of swords card depicts a scene filled with story: An skilled and confident thief is strolling some distance from a military camp with an armful of swords. He believes he's pulled it off, but in the left-hand historical beyond of the cardboard, it's miles smooth that some of the squaddies have observed him.

Upright: Deception and trickery in order to fast be placed out. A state of affairs in which you or someone else has felt the want to cowl some issue. This does no longer communicate of the morals of the person in question— there are times in existence even as a truth want to be hidden virtually for self-preservation. Unfortunately, this card indicates that the hidden truth will quick be found out. Take a message from the mind-set of the thief inside the card—they are sneaking away, seeking to be elusive. Perhaps it's time in an effort to face the tune and take the honest method, and then with a chunk of excellent fortune, have tons much less complex effects.

Reversed: Renewal of behavior, a coming domestic to honesty and honoring truth. Alternatively, it can searching for recommendation from a maliciously devious individual or conduct.

The Eight Of Swords

In this card, a lady is effective and blindfolded, surrounded through way of a 1/2 of-cage of swords. The desolate landscape mirrors her emotions. She want to without trouble stroll out of this entrapment, but she cannot see that freedom is some footsteps away.

Upright: Feeling victimized and powerless. Wallowing in self-pity or beaten thru disgrace, loss, or grief. The emotions which you haven't any alternatives left are making your scenario

worse. Take a threat and allow wish to re-input your mind. Alternatively, you could have willingly surrendered your power to some distinct employer company, be it spiritual, civic, or someone on your existence or to your dating. You want to benefit that electricity yet again as a manner to attain fulfillment.

Reversed: Reversed, this card is a exquisite omen. It way that you or the hassle of the studying are regaining a number of their non-public energy. It also way regained self belief, renewal of preference, and the exercise of one's strength with remarkable effects.

The Nine Of Swords

A woman sits bolt-upright in bed, her face blanketed with the aid of her hands. Nine swords shine towards the black wall at the back of her, representing fears, belongings of hysteria, and nightmares.

Upright: The story that every one started with the 8 of swords maintains proper right here. You were launched by using way of your self-imposed imprisonment, however the experience no matter the truth that haunts you. Anxiety and phobias. Bad reminiscences returning to preserve-out us.

Reversed: While trauma continues to have an effect on us, choice is on the horizon.

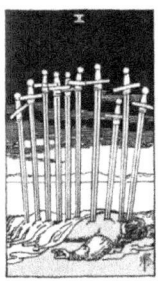

The Ten Of Swords

This some other card that can be quite annoying to get in a reading. A parent lies useless upon a nightmarish panorama; ten swords have pierced their body. Bizarrely, there may be a peaceful nature to the card. In the gap, the solar nevertheless rises.

Upright: You have reached the bottom element, and it can only get better from right here on up. Alternatively, an incredibly annoying occasion is poised to arise. Once it has handed, you will be capable of see the dawn and glide onward collectively along with your existence. The symbolism of the sword is -fold—the blades may be wielded as weapons, however they will be furthermore representational of thoughts and idea. If you made the mistake some of the figures inside the gambling playing cards preceding to this one did—conceitedness, gloating, deception, then this card is probably the end end result of your mistakes. Using records for growth, and no longer as a weapon, may be a better route so one can take.

Chapter 6: Simple Tarot Spreads

Preparing The Deck And Workspace

Tarot gambling playing cards are usually stored wrapped in material or a silk or velvet drawstring bag, to shield them from the energies of others. You might also moreover energize your tarot decks with crystals, or beneath the complete moon's moderate.

The ground upon that you do your studying, mainly if it's in a public or community location, must have a buffer located on it so the lingering energies of others who've been there in advance than you received't have an effect on the playing playing playing cards. A cloth unfold at some stage in a table works well. If the floor is in your property, a spray and wipe-down with Florida water, rose petal water, orange water, or a exquisite smoke of sage will assist easy the strength so that you can simply hobby on the playing gambling cards.

Shuffling And Cutting The Deck

Hold the deck of gambling playing cards on your hand, and faucet the again of them collectively collectively with your other hand, 3 times. This activates and awakens the playing playing cards.

Next, shuffle the deck very well. It doesn't simply depend the manner you accomplish this, so long as they're combined nicely. Some need to unfold a whole deck spherical on the workspace, transferring their arms in circles to spin and sincerely combo up the playing playing playing cards in advance than gathering them once more into an organized deck. If you don't want any reversal playing cards, of path, do not use this method.

Separate the deck into halves, and region one half of on top of the opportunity. Some readers pick out that the querent do that. After some instances, the deck is ready for the analyzing.

1. Past, Present, And Future Spread

There are three one-of-a-kind stages to this unfold: Beginner, intermediate, and advanced.

Beginner: As you shuffle and cut your deck, popularity to your existence as it's far now. Pretend which you are a looking a movie of your life—permit scenes from the beyond, present, and future to glide via your mind.

Once you've shuffled and reduce your deck, you can each pick out the card on pinnacle of the deck, then the subsequent two following that, or you may spread the playing playing cards in the course of your desk and choose out three random gambling cards. Place the playing playing cards you picked in a line: 1, 2, then 3.

1. Card One – The Past

As a fashionable rule, if the card you've selected is a primary arcana card, it issues a number one event or longer time frame. On a bit of paper, write the primary impressions that come to thoughts whilst you spot this card. Next, write a listing of additives of your existence which you are succesful to connect with the cardboard. Wait until you've performed this with every card earlier than you consult this e-book for delivered which means that.

2. Card Two – The Present

Flip the cardboard over and make a listing of first impressions, observed with the aid of using strategies you believe you studied this card connects to your life.

3. Card Three – The Future

Flip this card over and quit your list of first impressions, discovered with the aid of the usage of components which you count on this card connects to your existence. Next, searching for advice from this e-book's meanings. Draw strains to attach the impressions and record your final mind approximately what the playing cards are telling you.

For the intermediate model, separate your tarot deck into piles: One for the maximum arcana and one for the minor. For each step— beyond, gift, and future—select out one primary arcana card, then upload a minor arcana card to offer further due to this.

Chapter 7: Quick Reference Guide To Tarot Card Meanings

Major Arcana

zero The Fool: Beginnings, sparkling starts offevolved offevolved offevolved, optimism, faith, youthfulness, enthusiasm. Reversed: Delays, blind naïveté.

1 The Magician: Action, masterful energy, masculine energy, arcane facts, the potential to seem your desires.

Reversed: Miscommunications, impotence, charlatans, fakes.

2 The High Priestess: Making no motion, withdrawal, mysteries, secrets and techniques and techniques and techniques of the unconscious thoughts, magic and the occult, girl mystery, inner circles. Reversed: A manipulative person, pretense, smoke monitors, obfuscation.

three The Empress: Fertility and nurturing, abundance, the height of summer time, assets, recuperation, maternity and the mother goddess, creativity.

Reversed: A lawn neglected, withdrawn affection, infertility.

4 The Emperor: A established lifestyles, tremendous stability, prolonged-status traditions, sticking to the rules.

Reversed: Disorder, anarchy, the breakdown of the fame quo, insurrection.

five The Hierophant: The company of marriage, in addition to faith, societal traditions, law, courtesy and manners.

Reversed: A chaotic existence, elopement, redefining conventional roles.

6 The Lovers: Romantic love, sexual union, the presenting of options, duality, harmony.

Reversed: Withdrawal and separation, a parting of techniques, inequality.

7 The Chariot: Forward momentum, regular improvement, positivity, masculine energy.

Reversed: The want to give up, losing steam, lack of progress.

8 Strength: Compassion, acts of braveness, tempering violence with understanding. Reversed: Cowardice, crippling tension, timidity, worry.

nine The Hermit: The need to withdraw for first-rate skills, studies, mirrored image, contemplation, meditation. The chrysalis in advance than the butterfly.

Reversed: Forced isolation, banishment.

10 Wheel of Fortune: Cycles of existence, natural and first-rate exchange, opportunities, riding the typhoon to a powerful recovery.

Reversal: Ennui and stagnancy. The refusal to develop. Decay.

11 Justice: Law, karma, balanced forces, equality.

Reversed: Deceit, injustice, corruption.

12 The Hanged Man: Voluntary provider, surrendering to destiny and the herbal tactics of life, enlightenment, facts, persevered research.

Reversed: Refusal to alternate, lack of understanding, sullen vanity.

thirteen Death: An end that symptoms a starting, a super and sudden trade.

Reversed: A pause, being caught in a rut, a pressured stagnation.

14: Temperance: Measured stability, the entirety moderately, sobriety, sensibility.

Reversed: Addiction, codependency, lack of endurance.

15 The Devil: Material topics, dependancy, loss of private electricity.

Reversed: Regaining control, mastery of self.

16 The Tower: Great catastrophic however critical exchange, release, epiphany, awakening.

Reversed: A refusal to trade. Being stuck in a rut.

17 The Star: Hope, the universe achieving out to you, an auspicious signal. Reversed: Hopelessness, depression, darkness in advance than the sunrise.

18 The Moon: Magic and the occult, mysteries, the subconscious mind, subjects discovered in goals.